Don't Hold Your Poo-Poo

Written By
Sydney Adeniyi

Illustrated By
Surajit Gupta

To request permission, contact the publisher at dhys@thatguysydney.com

ISBN 979-8-9880397-5-4
ISBN 979-8-9880397-4-7 (pbk)
ISBN 979-8-9880397-6-1 (digital)

Written by Sydney Adeniyi
Illustrations by Surajit Gupta
Cover Art by Surajit Gupta & Sydney Adeniyi

Publisher website: www.dontholdyoursh.com

To my family, friends, and anyone who needs to let go.

Oh, Baby, what's wrong?

Baby has to go, but
Baby holds it in.
It hurt before and Baby can't
let go!

Don't hold your poo-poo,
you have to let go.
Baby says "No, no, no, I don't
want to go!"

Holds poo-poo
in, squeezing
head to toe!

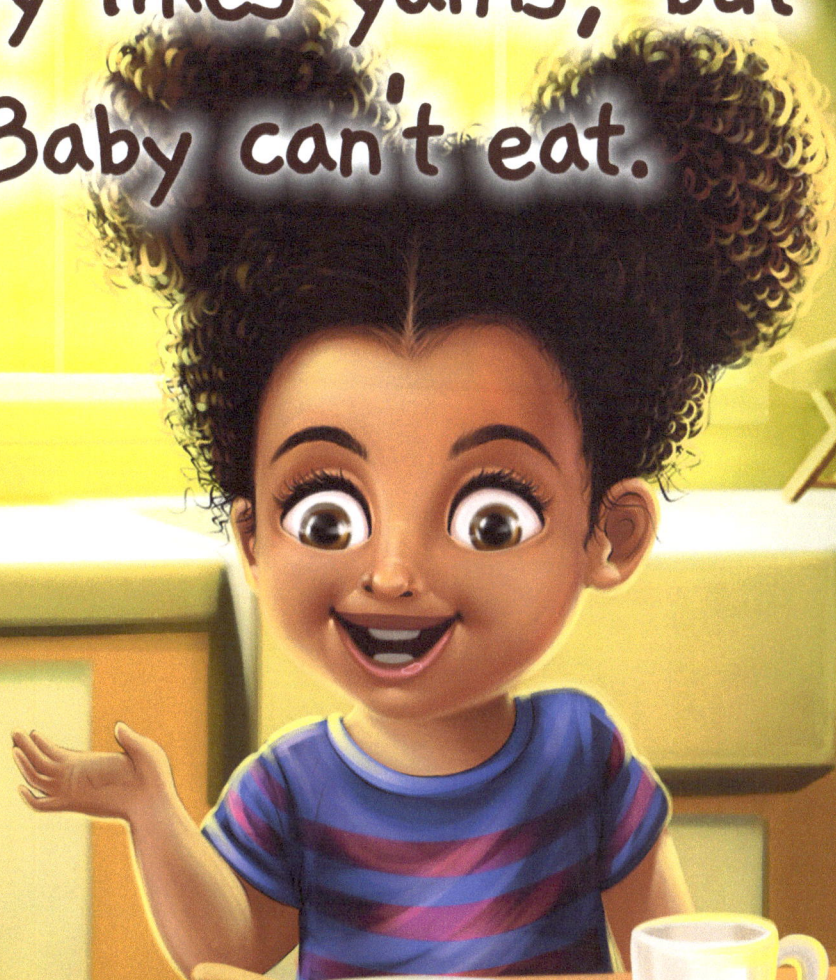

Baby likes yams, but
Baby can't eat.

Baby has to go and
tummy says no.

Don't hold your poo-poo, you have to let go.

Baby says "Arghhh! I don't want to go!" Holds poo-poo in, green starts to show!

Baby wants daycare, but Baby can't play. Baby has to go and has FOMO!

Don't hold your poo-poo,
you have to let go.

Baby says
"Unh-uh, I won't go!"

Holds poo-poo in,
about to blow!

Baby wants to share, but hurt-O!

Baby hurts friends when they come close.

Don't hold your poo-poo,
you have to let go.

Baby says
"Arghhh, no no no!"

Holds poo-poo in,
doing the most.

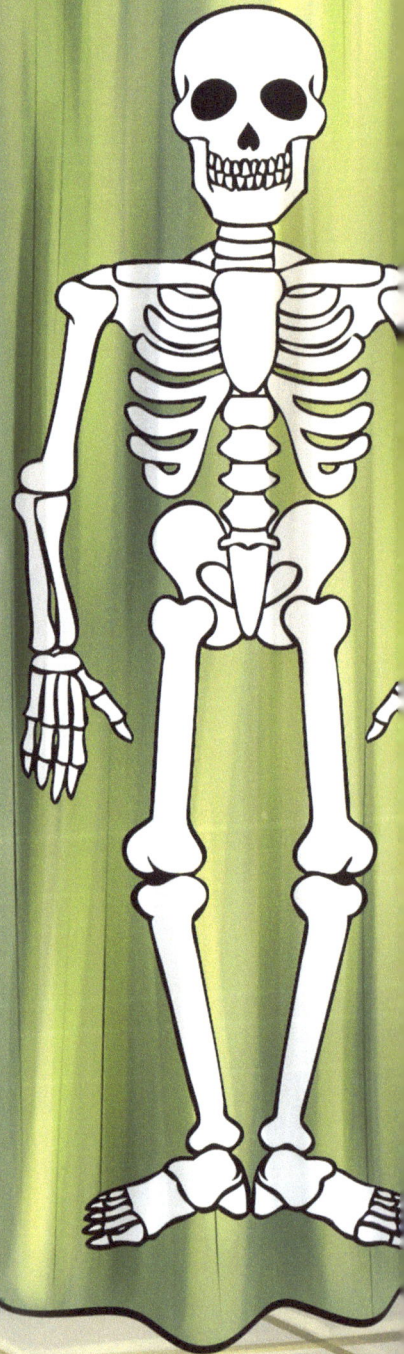

Just let it go!

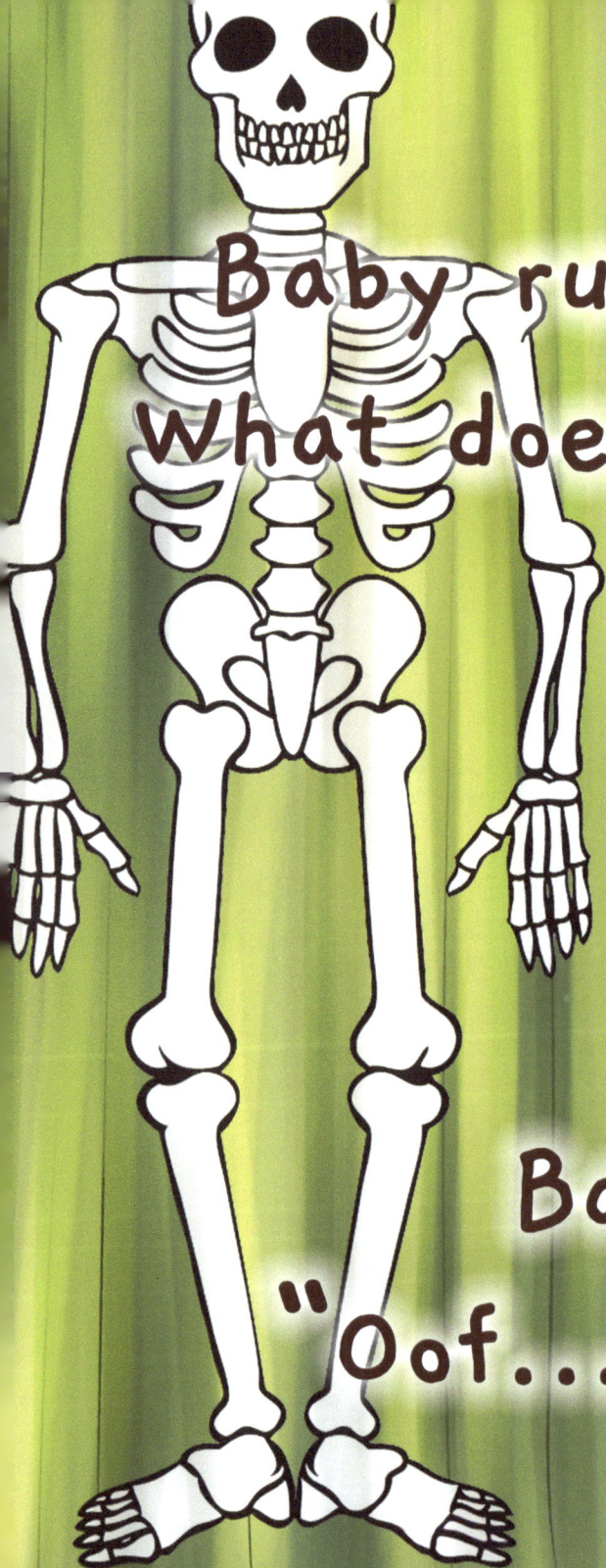

Baby runs and hides.
What does doctor know?

Baby says
"Oof... Oh no no!"

Holds poo-poo in
and starts to glow.

Sometimes hurt comes from friends, family, or food.

But Baby let it go
if you want to grow.

Don't hold your poo-poo,
you have to let go.

Baby says "No, no, nooo!"

Holds poo-poo in...

but poo-poo starts to flow.

Baby lets go...

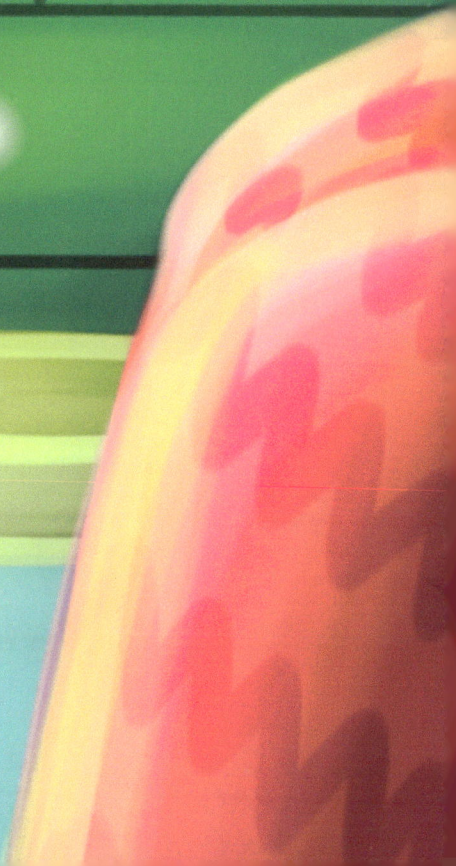

and poo-poos like a pro!

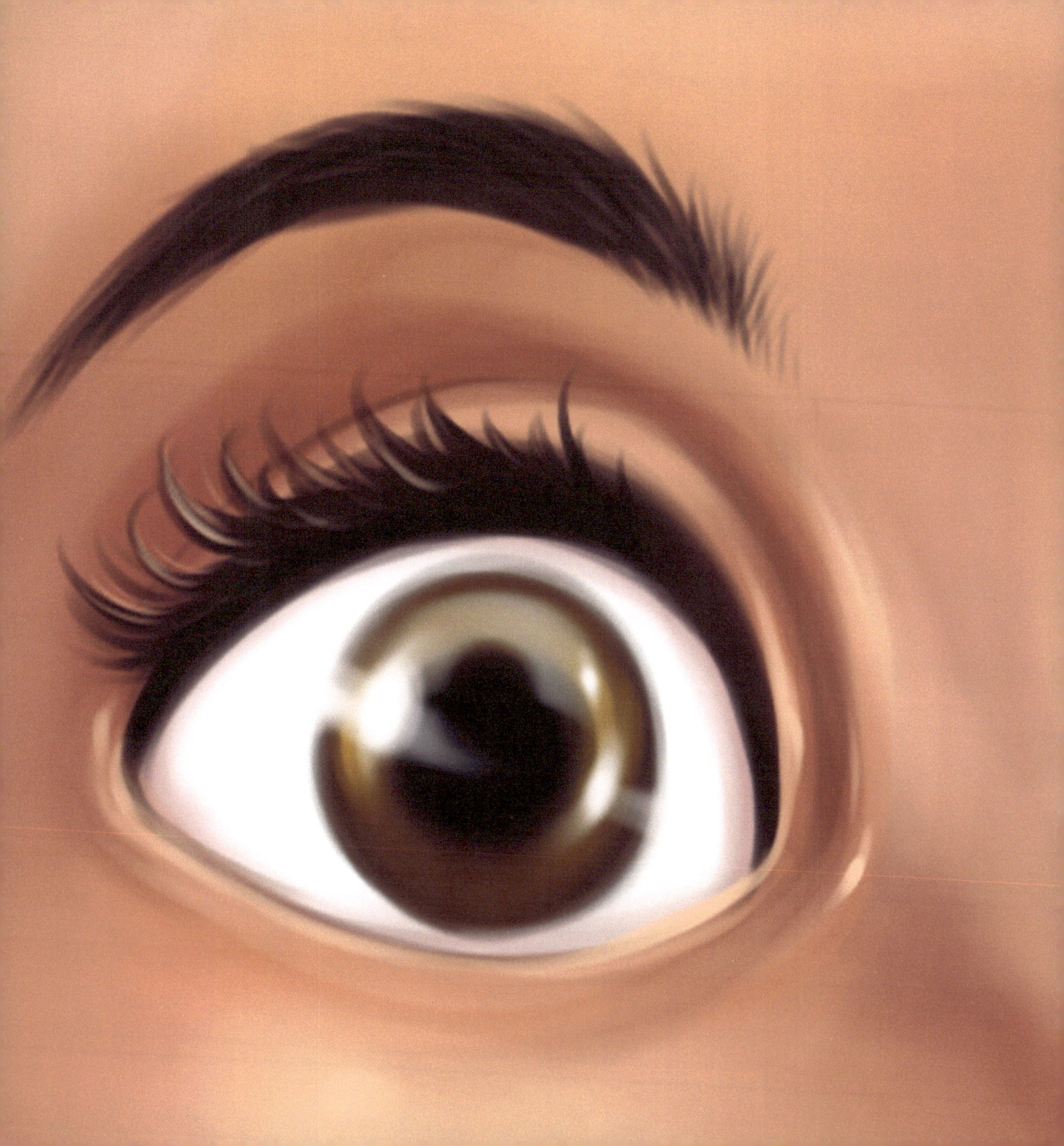

Letting go...

Look, we all have to poo-poo. Sometimes it's scary, especially if it hurt when we tried to go potty before. But holding it in, or hiding, or pretending we don't have to go will only make it hurt more. It's hard to have fun and play with our friends when our tummy hurts. The only way to feel good and get back to playing is by letting go and getting all the poo-poo out!

About the Author

Sydney Adeniyi is a stand-up comic, actor, and writer who is passionate about mental health. He has worked for Big Brothers Big Sisters, volunteered at Head Start, and performed at colleges across the US. He is also a Laughter On Call comedian who fosters mental wellness and connection for both working professionals and memory care residents. Sydney's unique comedy writings encourage psychological safety, inclusion, and equity.

www.ingramcontent.com/pod-product-compliance
Lightning Source LLC
Chambersburg PA
CBHW041553040426
42447CB00002B/173